SO *YOU* THINK YOU'VE GOT IT BAD?

A KID'S LIFE IN ANCIENT GREECE

nosy crow

First published 2019 by Nosy Crow Ltd
The Crow's Nest, 14 Baden Place,
Crosby Row, London SE1 1YW
www.nosycrow.com

978 1 78800 136 6 (HB)
978 1 78800 479 4 (PB)

Nosy Crow and associated logos are trademarks
and/or registered trademarks of Nosy Crow Ltd.

Published in collaboration with the British Museum.

Text © Chae Strathie 2019
Illustrations © Marisa Morea 2019

The right of Chae Strathie to be identified as the author and Marisa Morea
to be identified as the illustrator of this work has been asserted.

A CIP catalogue record for this book is available from the British Library.

Printed in China.
Papers used by Nosy Crow are made from wood
grown in sustainable forests.

1 3 5 7 9 8 6 4 2 (HB)
1 3 5 7 9 8 6 4 2 (PB)

SO *YOU* THINK **YOU'VE** *GOT IT* **BAD?**

A KID'S LIFE IN
ANCIENT GREECE

QUACK!

QUACK!

CONTENTS

CLOTHES AND HAIRSTYLES

Have you ever been given a totally weird haircut because the hairdresser sneezed at the wrong moment — leaving your head looking like a cross between a toilet brush and a sad hedgehog?

Or been standing there, picking your nose, when **WEDGER WATSON** and his gang appeared from nowhere? (You know full well what happens next. He didn't get that name for nothing!)

Yep, that's right. You've been given the world's worst **WEDGIE!**

Well if you think *YOU'VE* GOT IT BAD, at least you HAVE pants . . .

What will I wear today? The tunic, the tunic, or the tunic? Actually, I think I'll wear the tunic for a change.

Back in ancient Greece you would have had **NO SUCH THING**, just a loose tunic covering your **BARE BITS**. On the plus side that would have meant the Greek version of Wedger Watson — **WEDGENYSUS WATSITOTLE** — would have had nothing to **YANK** up to your **ARMPITS**.

On the downside, it was probably **A BIT BREEZY**, especially in winter.

FANCY THAT!
It was the job of girls and women to make clothes for the family. Luckily no fiddly cutting was required as only single strips of cloth were used for outfits.

What do you mean underwear hasn't been invented yet?

This is great! So fresh. So breezy!

Girls and women wore a long dress called a **PEPLOS**, which was a loose garment with a belt around the middle.

Boys wore a knee-length linen **TUNIC**, which was shorter than the one men wore.

Nudity was also considered **COMPLETELY NORMAL** for young men (OK, not **ALL** the time, but definitely when they were training in the gymnasium or competing in a sporting event). So if you're **KIND OF KEEN** on wearing trousers in public, probably best **AVOID** going back to ancient Greek times if you can possibly help it.

Careful where you're putting that pin — OUCH!

Very wealthy people could afford to buy expensive silks from the East, but even posh folk didn't have **ZIPS OR BUTTONS** — because there were **NO SUCH THINGS**. People just used pins, cords, belts or brooches to fasten their clothes.

Gulp!

In winter, goat skins could be used to make warmer clothes. Winter **WASN'T** a great time to be a goat.

Judging by traces of paint that have been found on statuettes, sculptures and painted pottery, clothes in ancient Greece were often brightly coloured. But how did they get the colours?

Why, SNAILS OF COURSE! (Talk about a silly question.)

The purple dyes, which were particularly prized, came from WATER SNAILS and . . . wait for it . . . INSECT LARVAE. That's right – WRIGGLY, SLIMY BABY BUGS.

Hey, I just LOVE your new dress. What colour is it?

Maggot!

Other dyes were made from plants, which is significantly LESS DISGUSTING. Yellow was a favourite colour among girls.

I feel sick.

FANCY THAT!

Women liked to lighten their skin by applying a special mixture of lead and vinegar. They also used seaweed as make-up and highlighted their eyebrows with charcoal. So if your mum smelled of vinegar and seaweed, she wasn't actually weird!

Like ancient Greek clothing, footwear was also simple. There were NO TRAINERS, BASEBALL BOOTS or WELLIES. They did have boots, shoes, and sandals though, and even wore socks to keep their toes toasty. Sandals and socks anyone?

ANCIENT FASHION FAIL!

But what about your noggin? What was going on up there?

Well . . . when it came to hair, both girls and boys often had long hair, which was sometimes braided.

Your dad and grandad would usually have a beard and shorter hair, while your mum would most likely have had her long hair tied up in a bun and sometimes covered with a scarf or veil, or even an ancient kind of granny-style hairnet.

Women sometimes also perfumed their hair with scented oils, which **SMELLED GREAT** but meant their favourite hats were always **SLIPPING OFF** their heads and landing on the ground with an **OILY PLOP**. Not a cool look.

IMPORTANT NOTE!
PLEASE DON'T try perfuming your hair with OIL from a pan that's been used to FRY SAUSAGES. It won't end well — although cats will suddenly find your head IRRESISTIBLE!

Do you ever wish...
you could compete in the Olympic Games?

Well, at least these days you wouldn't expect to be covered head to toe in olive oil . . . or run about stark naked! In the Olympic Games of ancient Greece (they came up with the idea) both of those things were completely normal.

It wasn't at all like the jolly and fairly risk-free running, jumping and throwing things we enjoy today. The ancient Greeks loved a bit of pain and danger.

Take horse racing. The jockeys rode without stirrups or saddles — so taking a tumble would just be part of the job. Then there was the *pankration*, which was a mixture of boxing and wrestling. Almost anything was allowed, although gouging an opponent's eyes and biting were frowned on.

Athletes mainly came from wealthy families, as only people who were stinking rich could afford to devote enough time to training. No women or slaves could compete. Oh, and forget medals — only the winners got prizes, while runners-up got nothing.

FAMILY LIFE

Families can be pretty annoying, right? Let's make a list of the ways families can drive you completely round the twist . . .

1) **MUM**: Makes you tidy your room even though there are **ONLY** 16 pairs of smelly socks, two broken skateboards and a mountain of mouldy mac 'n' cheese on the floor. What is her **MAJOR PROBLEM?**

2) **DAD**: Does "dad dancing" at every opportunity, tells "dad jokes" that stink more than a badger's bum, does bottom burps that stink more than his jokes.

3) **BIG SISTER**: Squeezes spots in your direction, trips you up as a hobby, blames **YOU** for everything from stealing her stuff to flooding the bathroom.

4) **LITTLE BROTHER**: Follows you **LITERALLY EVERYWHERE**, smells weird, steals all your stuff and is probably to blame for flooding the bathroom.

But if you think *YOU'VE* **GOT IT BAD**, get a load of this!

In ancient Greece, things could be **GRIM — REALLY GRIM**. Right from the moment you were born in fact. **WARNING TO GIRLS**: you may begin to feel **QUITE ANNOYED** about things as you read on.

Babyhood was a risky time, you see. In some ancient Greek states, unwanted babies, especially girls (sorry, we did warn you), were abandoned and left to die. It was more common for girls to be abandoned, simply because it was more expensive to have a girl. Parents had to provide a dowry (payment) when they got married.

Weak or poorly babies and those born to slaves were also in danger. Even those tiny tots who weren't left to fend for themselves had to face disease and illness as they grew up — in fact, probably as many as one in four babies died during their first year.

Not exactly a **LAUGH-A-MINUTE COMEDY** back in those days, eh?

FANCY THAT!

In Athens three and four-year-olds took part in a spring festival and tasted wine for the first time. If you have a little brother or sister, you'll know they're enough trouble without adding wine!

Note to self: next year tell Mum a flower headband is FINE.

On a happier, **LESS DEAD-Y**, note family life wasn't all bad. For instance, both girls and boys older than three took part in spring festivals in Athens, where they were **COVERED** in wild flowers to welcome the new season.

For kids growing-up in ancient Greece, the way of life for rich and poor children was very different.

Rich families had slaves to do **ALL** their work for them, and boys would go to school when they were seven, although – **SURPRISE, SURPRISE** – girls **DIDN'T** get to go. Instead, girls from rich families were educated at home, and had music and dance lessons at the temples.

The sons of poorer families would usually learn the trade of their father. For instance, a potter's son would be taught the skills of pot making.

But Dad, I want to be an astronaut when I grow up!

Family life nowadays includes being **DRAGGED TO THE SHOPS** against your will by your **CRUEL, HEARTLESS PARENTS**. But back then you wouldn't be **TRUDGING** round a **SUPERMARKET** with a trolley. Shopping was done at a market around the *agora*, which was a bustling, lively place where people met at the centre of towns.

There were **NO BURGER RESTAURANTS** anywhere, so no amount of **BLEATING** would get you a meal with the latest plastic figure of Zeus as the free toy.

I have *literally* no idea what you are talking about. Have an olive.

Muuuuum! I wanna Cheerful Meal!

Slaves were sold at market. You could inspect them and pick one you thought would be a good worker. Imagine how that must have felt for the slaves.

Another downside for girls was the fact they were often married as young as 13 — and may never even have met their husband before the wedding.

Somehow being **NAGGED** to **PICK UP YOUR SOCKS** and listening to your dad's **STINKY OLD JOKES** doesn't seem quite as bad now . . .

REALLY STINKY SOCKS

Do you ever wish . . . you had someone to do all the stuff you don't like doing?

Well many ancient Greeks had just that. But it wasn't a good thing — in fact, it was very bad! The Greeks of ancient times relied on slaves to carry out lots of jobs. As many as one third of the population of Athens was made up of slaves!

Slaves were usually treated as "property" under Athenian law. They could be bought, sold, and beaten (but only by their master — as if that makes it any better). While many slaves worked in family houses, others mastered crafts and many worked in the silver mines of Laurion.

There was also a holiday especially for slaves, called the *Kronia*. On that day state business was stopped and slaves dined with their masters. It sounds about as much fun as having dinner with your teacher!

Although life was tough for many people back then, it didn't get any tougher than for slaves.

Every family needs a pet or seven, right? So what kinds of FURRY FRIENDS did ancient Greek kids keep?

Well, it turns out the ancient Greeks **DIDN'T KEEP CATS** as pets **AT ALL**. Moggies were sometimes used as pest control on farms and ships, but most people preferred to use **FERRETS** to catch mice and rats instead.

What they **DID** have were **DOGS**. Among ancient Greeks, the dog was by far the **TOP PET**. Many vase-paintings show that children were particularly attached to their **BARKING BUDDIES**. In one music-school scene, a boy appears to have just **PLAYED A LYRE** for his pet's enjoyment.

Have you ever tried playing guitar for your **PET POODLE**?

Do it now!

But if you fancy something a bit more **OFF THE WALL**, some ancient Greeks even kept **MONKEYS** or **CHEETAHS** as pets. So much so that some people were said to **PREFER MONKEYS TO CHILDREN!**

Can you blame them? Have you seen the state of your bedroom?

FANCY THAT!

King Alexander the Great was given his horse, Bucephalus, at the age of 12. No adult could control it, but Alexander realised that the horse was frightened of its own shadow, so he calmed it by turning its head to the sun. If your pet gerbil is a bit jittery, why not try the same thing?

SNAKES were kept in ancient households to eat vermin and mice, and possibly NAUGHTY KIDS — so WATCH OUT!

Where is everybody?

Even a type of chirping insect called a CICADA (a bit like a grasshopper) was kept as a pet. The Greeks reckoned they were as LOVELY to listen to as SINGING BIRDS and kept them in little cages. Talk about WEIRD.

GOATS, SWANS, DUCKS, and GEESE were also favourite pets — in fact the last two were almost as popular as the dog.

Speaking of which, have you taken your goose out for a walk today?

QUACK!

QUACK!

THE HOME

Ever feel a bit grumbly about your house? It's not big enough. It's not shiny and cool, it doesn't have a games room, the lights aren't voice-activated and there are no robot butlers *at all!*

Well stop whining, **YOU WHINY WHINEMITTEN** from the **PLANET WHINEPLOP-Z**.

If you think *YOU'VE* **GOT IT BAD**, spare a thought for the ancient Greeks – they had **NO GLASS** in their windows, poor people lived in houses made of **BAKED MUD** and there were exactly **ZERO TOILETS** – even for the super-rich!

That's right, you had to **POO IN A POT**.

Welcome to ancient Greece!

FANCY THAT!

One vase painting shows a little boy sitting in a tall potty which also seems to double as a high chair. Sounds great – no need to leave the table when you need to go to the toilet! Just think of the time you'd save.

A lot of homes had a courtyard at the centre of them, while the outside walls had small windows high up. The Greeks CLEARLY liked their privacy (despite the whole NAKEDNESS thing).

Many homes had an ALTAR to the gods ZEUS and APOLLO. When the family prayed together they offered a gift to the gods. It could be A CAKE, A BIRD or A SHEEP.

Hoi! Are you the god Zeus or Apollo??

Errr, no. I just love honey fudge cake.

What kind of rooms would you find inside an ancient Greek house? Let's go inside and take a look . . .

GYNAIKON

KITCHEN

ANDRON

WATER CLOCK

COURTYARD

The **BIGGEST** room in a typical Greek house was called **THE ANDRON**.
This was where the men had **PARTIES. NO WOMEN** were allowed.

BEDROOMS

One place women **WERE ALLOWED** was **THE KITCHEN**, which had a **BIG FIRE** in the middle of the room for cooking. When the women were not cooking they were often **SPINNING** and **WEAVING**. They had their own area in the house called the **GYNAIKON**, which is also where the children would play.

Most women and girls were not allowed to do much in ancient Greece except **WORK** and . . . err, that's it. I know. **IT SOUNDS RUBBISH!** Please do not take it out on this book by **THROWING IT OUT OF THE WINDOW, BURYING** it in a hole or **FEEDING IT TO A COW.**

BATHROOMS

ALTAR

If your mum told you to have a **BATH** before bed there were several ways to get clean. Rich people's houses might have a **SEPARATE BATHROOM** with a **CLAY BATH** and a drain leading outside. Poorer homes would have had a more basic basin for washing in.

Many ancient Greek houses had bedrooms, but they didn't always have beds. So where *DID* our ancient Greek friends sleep?

Yaaaawn. I feel tired. Pass the parsley – I think it's thyme for a snooze.

It turns out they slept on Greek couches, which doubled up as beds. They probably WOULDN'T have been VERY COMFY, with animal skins to lie on and a simple blanket to cover you. You may NOT have EVEN had a pillow.

Depending on what period you were living in the ancient Greek world, and how poor you were, you may also have slept ON THE FLOOR on straw or DRIED HERBS. And no, we don't recommend sprinkling A TUB OF OREGANO from your kitchen cupboard on floor next time you feel like a nap.

BED OF HERBS

OLIVE OIL

STRIGIL

If your house DIDN'T have easy access to water, a totally NON-WET method of cleaning yourself was by RUBBING OLIVE OIL ALL OVER YOUR BODY and then SCRAPING it off, along with dirt and dust, with a special scraping tool called A STRIGIL.

GREASY and SCRATCHY. GROSS!

At least you got to have a nice bath afterwards to wash off all the grime.

FANCY THAT!

A water clock uses flowing water to measure time. Either a container is filled with water, and the water is drained out slowly and evenly, or water slowly enters a container. In both cases you can tell how much time has passed depending on which line the water level is at.

One more thing — there were **NO PROPER CLOCKS** in those days so Greeks used **A SUNDIAL** or **A WATER CLOCK** to tell the time. Doesn't sound like a problem?

Well, there were **NO ALARM CLOCKS** either, which means being late for school, which means **PUNISHMENT EXERCISES**.

Every. Single. Day.

I am sooooooooo late!

Do you ever wish . . . your parents had an amazingly cool new car that could drive itself, fly in space and had an on-board chocolate fountain?

Well in ancient Greek times you were lucky if you had anything with wheels on at all! Back then the roads were rubbish and most people did not travel far from home at all.

Favourite mode of transport? Feet. You probably have a pair of those too. Check at the bottom of your legs. They're those pink things with wiggly bits on the end that smell of cheese.

Aside from foot-power, donkeys were the main mode of transport used by people for local travel and to take produce to market. Long journeys were made by boat to avoid the mountains.

There weren't many wheeled vehicles, although mules were used to pull two-wheeled carts and four-wheeled wagons. Horse-drawn chariots were used in warfare in Mycenaean times, but later on they were only used in sport.

There is a record of a chariot race at the Olympic Games in which 40 chariots took part. The winner was the only charioteer who managed to survive the race!

EDUCATION

Hands up if you love school. Two hands up if you don't love school. Seventeen hands up if you're a weird seventeen-headed alien who has infiltrated school to take over the brains of the pathetic humans and become their all-conquering overlord.

Whatever your thoughts on school, most people would agree that sometimes it can be a bit, well, **SCHOOLISH**. But if you think *YOU'VE* **GOT IT BAD**, it could be worse.

At least you get to **LEARN STUFF** — not all ancient Greeks were so lucky.

Guess who **DIDN'T** get to go school? No, **NOT SPIDERS**. The people who weren't allowed to become pupils were . . . girls. That's right — **GIRLS DID NOT GET TO GO TO SCHOOL**, although some rich girls did learn to read and write.

This doesn't seem fair. Especially as by the time they were **SEVEN OR EIGHT** girls were instead taught how to **RUN A HOME**.

Doing art lessons, working out sums and writing about what you did during the summer holidays seems like **MUCH** more fun.

Most boys in rich families went to school from around the age of seven. They had a slave called a **PEDAGOGUE** whose job was to take them to school, sit with them in lessons and make sure **THEY BEHAVED**. When they came home from school the pedagogue helped them with their homework.

Aside from the fact that having a slave is **EXTREMELY BAD**, how annoying would it be to have someone **CONSTANTLY HANGING AROUND** when you're trying to have fun with your pals?

Although the homework thing could come in handy . . .

FANCY THAT!

Pythagoras was a great ancient Greek mathematics thinker and teacher: the theories he came up with are still taught today. But he also believed that beans had souls, so he told his students never to eat them! Next time you chomp a plate of beans, listen out in case they squeal . . .

Hurry up, you've got to do my Greek homework next

So, what kind of AWESOME and BRILLIANT things did ancient Greek kids get to learn about at school?

POETRY, of course! Boys (who were the only type of ancient Greek kid you would find in schools) learned to read and write, and spent a lot of time focusing on the work of a great poet called HOMER (no, he has NOTHING the do with *The Simpsons*).

They learned his poems about GODS, HEROES and BATTLES in far-off lands by heart — which is QUITE IMPRESSIVE considering they are EXTREMELY LONG. In fact, one of them called *The Iliad* is a brain-bending 15,693 LINES IN LENGTH!

If you have trouble remembering SIMPLE THINGS like your name and what a banana is for, then this may have been a struggle for you.

Boys also learned to SING and play the FLUTE, LYRE (which looked like a strange guitar) and HARP.

When it came to taking notes in lessons, a pen and paper would have baffled our ancient Greek friends. They wrote on **WOODEN TABLETS** covered in **SOFT WAX** that was scratched on with a small stick-like implement called **A STYLUS**, usually made of bone or metal.

Just in case you were getting all excited, a tablet in ancient times was a block of wood or stone, **NOT** an **ELECTRONIC DEVICE** for watching funny videos of cats on. **SOZ**.

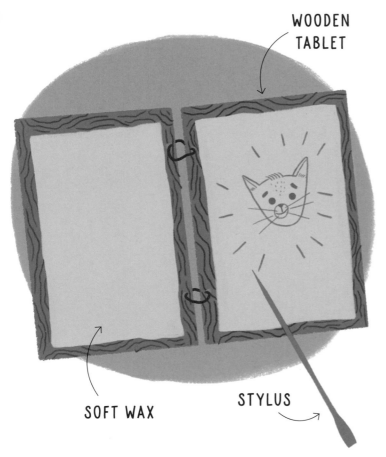

WOODEN TABLET

SOFT WAX

STYLUS

FANCY THAT!

Ancient Greek boys went to school from about the ages of 7 to 13 and studied maths, reading, writing, music, dance, astronomy, rhetoric (public speaking and debating) and philosophy. Most boys then continued to study at military school until they were about 20 years old. But they had to watch out. If they didn't learn fast enough, their tutors would beat them with a stick. Ouch!

Do you ever wish . . .

you could ditch the paint in art class and create something a bit more, well, impressive?

Greek sculptors made beautiful lifelike figures of both people and gods. Some were found in temples and some were placed outdoors. They were usually carved from marble or cast in bronze.

Statues were pretty much always of men, and guess what most of them weren't wearing? Yep – clothes. What was it with the ancient Greeks and bare bits?

Whoops!

Most Greek statues were painted in bright colours to make them more lifelike. Those that have survived to this day were carved from stone such as marble, which is hard and long-lasting, although some of the sticky-out bits have been snapped off or damaged . . . ouch!

Although most Greek paintings have not survived, pictures painted on vases, jugs, bowls and other types of pottery have. Many of these scenes have told us a lot of what we know about ancient Greek life.

Perhaps you should draw a picture of yourself pulling a funny face on a cereal bowl – just so people in the future know exactly what you were like?

If you try to work out early Greek writing, your brain might overheat, sending flames and smoke shooting out of your earholes! So why is it so hard to understand?

To begin with it went from RIGHT TO LEFT on the first line, then LEFT TO RIGHT on the next and so on.

AS YOU CAN SEE, !YKCIRT YREV SAW TI

By the 5th century BC, writing only moved from left to right, like ours . . . but it was all in CAPITAL LETTERS, had no spaces between the words and very little punctuation.

TRYWORKINGOUTWHATTHISSAYSWITHOUTYOUREYES GOINGFUNNYANDYOURHEADEXPLODING!

FANCY THAT!

In the Classical Period people wrote on papyrus — a plant which came from Egypt. Strips of it were pressed together to make sheets that were then glued together to make rolls up to 30 feet long with wooden rollers at each end. These were early "books". Not exactly handy if you like reading in bed without pulling a muscle.

Ummmm, hello?

As far as letters go, the ancient Greek ones were
pretty awesome. Each symbol also has a cool name.

GREEK LETTER	NAME OF GREEK LETTER	LETTER SOUND
Αα	Alpha	A
Ββ	Beta	B
Γγ	Gamma	G
Δδ	Delta	D
Εε	Epsilon	Short E
Ζζ	Zeta	Z
Ηη	Eta	AY
Θθ	Theta	TH
Ιι	Iota	I
Κκ	Kappa	K
Λλ	Lambda	L
Μμ	Mu	M
Νν	Nu	N
Ξξ	Xi	KS or X
Οο	Omicron	Short O
Ππ	Pi	P
Ρρ	Rho	R
Σσς	Sigma	S
Ττ	Tau	T
Υυ	Upsilon	OU
Φφ	Phi	PH
Χχ	Chi	Hard CH or K
Ψψ	Psi	PS
Ωω	Omega	Long O

To test your amazing new brain-busting cleverness, try working out what these words are . . .

ΜΕΓΑΛΟΠΟΛΙΣ   ΔΗΜΟΚΡΑΤΙΑ   ΑΘΛΟΣ

ONE LAST THING! Have you noticed anything about the word "alphabet"? (Clue: check out the first two letters of the Greek alphabet . . .)

ANSWERS: Megalopolis (a large city), Democracy (a system of voting for an elected leader), Prize (the word athlete also comes from this)

27

LIFE AS A SPARTAN

There's nothing worse than being EATEN BY A FOX. Actually, being slowly nibbled by a TINY KITTEN might be worse, because they're really small and cute and you'd look a bit silly if you couldn't even stop a kitten eating you.

Luckily, the closest you'll probably get is being bitten by a flea, which is EXTREMELY ANNOYING, but if you think *YOU'VE* GOT IT BAD, just say a BIG OLD THANK YOU that you're NOT growing up in Sparta . . .

FANCY THAT!

Spartan boy soldiers were not very well fed and if they were caught STEALING they were punished severely – not for stealing . . . but for being CAUGHT. There is a story about a Spartan boy who stole a FOX and hid it under his tunic. The animal gnawed into his body but the boy chose to die rather than wail out loud and be found out.

Sparta was one of the **MOST** important Greek city states outside of Athens, which was around 95 miles away as the crow flies. If you weren't a crow and had to walk it was **A LOT** further.

Life in Sparta was **EVER SO SLIGHTLY** on the **TOUGH** side. Just a **TEENY-TINY BIT**. You see, the Spartans had conquered another region called **LACONIA** and made the people slaves. But they were always worried the slaves might rebel so they trained their children to become **FIERCE WARRIORS**, just in case.

Perhaps more so than in other parts of Ancient Greece, babies that were considered **TOO WEAK** to grow into **TOUGH, FEARLESS SOLDIERS** were **LEFT OUTSIDE** to die. The boys who made it were moulded into warriors in the toughest ways.

Seriously, even being made to run twice around the playing field by your PE teacher isn't as bad as what the Spartan kids had to go through . . .

To become a Spartan warrior you had to be the TOUGHEST of the tough. So what exactly did training involve?

When a boy was **SEVEN** he left home to live in **A HARSH CAMP** in the mountains, where he learned to be **A BRAVE SOLDIER** and **AN ATHLETE**.

WRESTLING

HUNTING AND FISHING

MARCHING

STORYTELLING

STEALING FOOD

Do you ever wish . . . you got one BILLION dollars a week in pocket money?

Well, if you get any pocket money at all you should be thankful. You wouldn't have been so lucky in ancient Greek times — especially not if you lived in Sparta. The Spartans never developed coins, so you wouldn't have been given anything to put in your piggy bank in return for taking the bins out or whatever . . .

Other parts of ancient Greece did use coins, however. And if you got any of these in your pocket money you'd be jumping for joy. A clay jug filled with coins was found at the temple of Artemis at Ephesus and the coins were made of electrum, which is a mixture of gold and silver. Imagine how many jelly babies one of those could buy!

Before money came along, the ancient Greeks traded by exchanging goods of equal value, such as silver and axes. So if you happen to have any silver or axes kicking around under your bed, hang on to them. You never know when you might bump into an ancient Greek offering a cool skateboard as a swap.

As if this wasn't **BRUTAL** enough, at 11, training became **HARDER**. The boys were only given a cloak to wear (yet more **BARE BUMS** — how typically ancient Greek), hardly **EVER** had baths and slept on rough, uncomfortable beds.

Can you smell something weird?

Yes! It smells like fish, pig poop and crusty socks all rolled into one. What is it?

Us — we haven't had a bath since last year.

The Spartans reckoned **CORPORAL PUNISHMENT** (being whacked, whipped or beaten) was **GOOD** for a child's character. Young Spartans were also encouraged to fight one another, though never in anger, and **COWARDICE** was a crime.

Makes school sound like a right **BARREL OF GIGGLES**, doesn't it?

In Sparta, girls were treated more equally than anywhere else in ancient Greece.

About time too! Oh, wait . . .

FANCY THAT!

Girls in Sparta actually got to go to school, and also learned how to race horses and wrestle. There was even an all-female chariot racing competition. That sounds a bit more fun than weaving and baking bread!

Of course — that means they were treated equally HORRIBLY . . .

Although they WEREN'T sent off to Spartan training camps in the mountains like boys, girls had to train to be STRONG AND FIT athletes, and they raced with the boys during festivals.

Do you ever wish . . . your life was more exciting?

Well, in ancient Greece it could get pretty wild — though you may not have liked it much.

Warfare was a big part of life back then. In Athens boys trained as soldiers from when they left school, but in Sparta training began much earlier, and young boys would be turned into tough warriors through brutality and hardship. Sometimes they didn't even get a hot-water bottle or a teddy to cuddle.

If you were an ancient Greek child it's quite likely your dad or even grandad could be called on to fight in wars. Greek soldiers were called *hoplites* — which had nothing to do with jumping up and down on one leg (unless the other had been chopped off by an enemy soldier with a big sword).

In one statuette that's still around today, a Spartan girl is seen running in such a race. Her skirt was **MUCH SHORTER** than would have been allowed in other Greek cities, which shows another difference in how girls were viewed.

Although girls did not fight in wars, the Spartans wanted them to grow up to be strong and fit so they could give birth to **HEALTHY SONS** who would go on to become **TOUGH WARRIORS**.

Wealthy men had to pay for their own weapons and armour, and some even had horses, while poorer men served as hoplites armed with shields and spears, and the poorest were oarsmen in warships. These warships, called *triremes*, were powered by 170 oarsmen on three levels, one above the other. At the front was a ram covered in metal to smash into enemy ships and sink them. How much do you want one of THOSE at your local boating pond?

In Greek pictures warriors were sometimes depicted with no clothes on. Nakedness was a symbol of bravery in Greek art. It is not a symbol of bravery nowadays. We repeat, it is NOT a symbol of bravery nowadays.

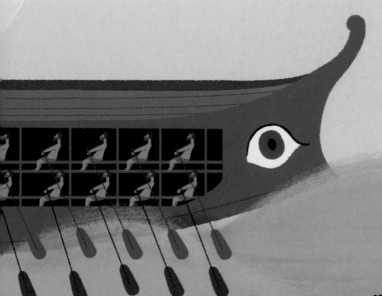

DIET

What scrummy delight do you have for lunch today? If you have a packed lunch, perhaps you have a limp cheese sandwich that's got a bit, you know, sweaty, after sitting in your bag in a hot classroom all morning. Mmmmm, sweaty cheese that tastes like a bogeyman's pants. Yum.

Or maybe you're getting lunch from the **SCHOOL CANTEEN**. You know, the one with the **EVIL-LOOKING DINNER LADY** who **SNEEZES** in the soup to give it extra flavour . . .

But if you think *YOU'VE* **GOT IT BAD**, stop grumbling and check this out.

At least you **HAVE** sandwiches, pasta, chips and the like to choose from. Back in ancient Greek times, there were fewer things on the menu . . . and some **PRETTY WEIRD** stuff.

SOGGY WINE-BREAD

> Soggy wine-bread or curdled milk and cheese pancakes?

To kick their day off ancient Greeks ate bread (so far, so normal) **DIPPED IN WINE!** For brekkie? **YUCKETY-YUCK!** Try concentrating on your sums in class after that.

> Errrr, are there any cornflakes? Toast and jam? A banana?

Another breakfast fave was **TEGANITES**, which were a bit like pancakes. If you think that sounds OK, they were made with wheat flour, olive oil, honey . . . and **CURDLED MILK!** They were topped with honey or, if you were rich, cheese. **BLEEEUUURRRGH!**

> Just a glass of water for me, thanks.

For lunch it was usually bread and a sort of rough goat's cheese made of – yep, **YOU GUESSED IT** – more curdled milk. **DELICIOUS**. If you like that sort of thing.

Dinner for most ancient Greeks would have been **FAIRLY** basic, depending on how rich you were and where you lived. In the country farmers had farm animals to eat, such as chickens, while people could also hunt hares and other wild animals.

People who lived close to the sea would have had easier access to fish, while in cities fish was expensive and seen as a luxury dish – as it was hard to transport fish and keep it fresh in the hot climate.

35

If you asked an ancient Greek what his favourite pizza topping was or whether he liked cheeseburgers or hotdogs best, he would just have stared at you for a moment . . . then ran away from the scary babbling weirdo (that's you, by the way).

Bread, vegetables and fruit made up the staple diet of most ancient Greeks, not **PROCESSED JUNK FOOD**, and there was no rice or potatoes. That's right. **NO CHIPS. EVER.** And if you **LOVE** a sausage, **BAD LUCK**. The ancient Greeks only ate red meat on special occasions, such as at weddings or religious festivals.

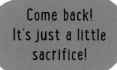
Come back! It's just a little sacrifice!

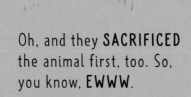
Oh, and they **SACRIFICED** the animal first, too. So, you know, EWWW.

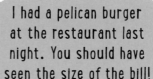
I had a pelican burger at the restaurant last night. You should have seen the size of the bill!

FANCY THAT!

All sorts of birds were eaten, particularly by the rich. Not just chickens, ducks and geese, like we eat today — oh no. They also chomped pigeons, sparrows, thrushes, swans and even, very occasionally, huge-beaked PELICANS!

Sadly there was always a danger of food shortages when not enough rain fell to water crops, so **DROUGHTS** and **FAMINE** were not uncommon. Makes you realise how lucky you really are, doesn't it?

> Looks like we'll be having dirt and water for dinner again.

Having said that, you might have preferred going without a meal or two in the city of Sparta. The tough old Spartans often ate a soup made from **PIGS' LEGS** and **BLOOD**.

Second helpings?

NO THANKS, we'll pass . . .

Do you ever wish . . .

you could spend all day relaxing and never have to help out at home?

Well count yourself lucky you're not an ancient Greek kid. Their chores might have included picking grapes if they lived in the country. They would then squish them with their bare feet to make wine and vinegar. Yeuch!

And it was even worse for girls. From a young age, they were taught household tasks like cooking and clothes-making. They had to work hard, although richer households had slaves to do a lot of the more difficult jobs.

In fact, children may not have been viewed all that differently from slaves. The ancient Greek word for child, "pais", can also mean slave!

Tidying your room isn't exactly on the same level, OK?

HEALTH AND MEDICINE

When you have a sniffle you probably think: "Oh dear, I have a sniffle." Then, depending on how much you want the day off school, you proceed to wail and flop about, snotting the place up and annoying everyone until your mum and dad give in and let you stay home . . .

Of course, within HALF AN HOUR you've "MIRACULOUSLY" recovered enough to play *BLOWING RANDOM STUFF UP 3* on the XBOX for the rest of the day. Which is why no one shows you ANY sympathy.

But if you think *YOU'VE* GOT IT BAD, at least you don't believe your tiny sniffle is a punishment from god!

The ancient Greeks thought illness was caused by the chief god ZEUS and his buddies being angry with them. To try to find a cure the sick would often visit the SANCTUARIES OF ASKLEPIOS, the god of medicine. They believed he would give them treatments through his priests and would hope to be visited by him in their sleep. CREEPY!

You want me to carve a WHAT?

Patients who thought they had been **CURED** by Asklepios often left a model of the part of the body that had been affected by illness. One marble carving that is still around today shows a leg and has an inscription to Asklepios on it.

Imagine you'd been **BITTEN ON THE BUM** by a **GRUMPY PELICAN**. That would be a **MIGHTY EMBARRASSING** request for the local carver!

Things changed when the Greek physician **HIPPOCRATES** came along. He believed illnesses had natural causes and worked out treatments after making detailed studies of the symptoms. He is often described as the founder of modern medicine, and doctors in some parts of the world still take what is called the "Hippocratic Oath", which means they promise to look after people well.

HIPPOCRATES

FANCY THAT!

The ancient Greeks believed in the power of magical prayers. We're not sure what magical prayer was used for the sniffles, but it was probably something along the lines of: "My throat is sore, my face is hot, my head is filled with bright green snot. I pray this sniffle quickly goes and gunk stops dripping from my nose".*

* This is an excellent magical prayer, but probably nothing like a real ancient Greek one.

Before the Greek physician Hippocrates came along — much of ancient Greek medicine relied on magical prayers, charms and the wearing of amulets. Special plants and herbs were also thought to have healing powers.

Unfortunately, **MAGIC AND CHARMS** aren't as effective as modern medicine, and so a lot of young ancient Greeks didn't make it to adulthood. If you managed to get through your first few years without being struck down by **HORRIBLE DISEASES**, your parents would be **PRETTY CHUFFED**.

Thank you, Zeus! Have a sheep.

When children were **THREE YEARS OLD** their father made a **SACRIFICE** to **ZEUS** and **ATHENA** to thank them for letting his children survive.

But of course, at some point it would be time to **POP OFF TO THE UNDERWORLD** (that's where ancient Greeks believed people went when they died).

Many people buried their dead, which took them closer to the underground kingdom of the dead, knocking a little bit of time off their journey and meaning they might get there in time for lunch.

While the poor were simply buried in the ground, the rich could afford something a little more elaborate. They had **TOMBS** which were decorated with pictures of their feats in life, like that time they **ATE A WHOLE SWAN** in one go and that other time they **DID A HANDSTAND** for **FIVE WHOLE MINUTES** without falling over.

FANCY THAT!

Around the fifth century BC, doctors thought illnesses were caused by an imbalance of fluids in the body, so "bloodletting" became popular. If you were feeling poorly, a doc would cut open one of your veins, letting blood flow out into a bowl. If you were REALLY lucky you might get a leech or three popped on to your body to suck the blood out! It's as gruesome as it sounds and guess what — it doesn't even work.

This won't hurt a bit . . .

LEECH

Actually, I've changed my mind. I feel better now!

41

Rich ancient Greeks sometimes buried their dead with their favourite possessions and food for the afterlife.

They wanted to make sure their dead relatives had EVERYTHING THEY NEEDED so they could enjoy a HAPPY NEW LIFE IN THE UNDERWORLD — a bit like going on a school trip, except you wouldn't come home with A NOVELTY PENCIL SHARPENER or SOUVENIR BASEBALL CAP. The things they buried usually included useful everyday objects such as bowls, combs, trinkets and food. Richer Greeks were buried with beautiful jewellery, furniture and other valuable objects.

Once the dead person reached their destination they had to pay **CHARON**, who was the ferryman who carried the dead across the **RIVER STYX** into the **UNDERWORLD**. The trip cost one *abol* (and no, you couldn't buy a return ticket) so the person's family sometimes left a coin on their body to pay for the journey.

CHARON was known for his rudeness, which was a bit uncalled for considering that his passengers would have already been having **A PRETTY BAD DAY**, what with all the **DEADNESS** and whatnot.

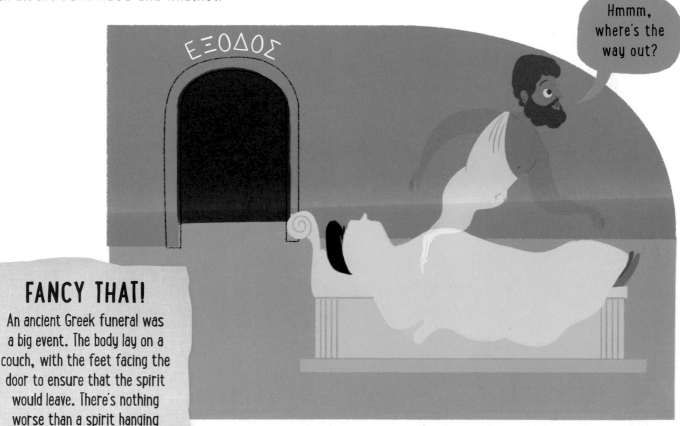

FANCY THAT!

An ancient Greek funeral was a big event. The body lay on a couch, with the feet facing the door to ensure that the spirit would leave. There's nothing worse than a spirit hanging around because the feet were facing the wardrobe by mistake.

Many Greeks believed that the dead person's soul rose up to become one of the stars before being reborn in a new body. Something to bear in mind next time you're out alone on a dark starry night!

MYTHS AND LEGENDS

Do you like telling people about the amazing things you and your family have done? Like that QUEST you and your dad went on to defeat the Beast with FOURTEEN BOTTOMS and BIG POINTY TEETH?

And who can forget your GRANDMA'S journey to the CAVE OF ARRGGHH to find the LOST MOUSTACHE OF DESTINY? The only problem is, of course, that everyone thinks you're just a little teller of BIG FIBS.

But if you think *YOU'VE* GOT IT BAD, the tall tales that were told in ancient Greece REALLY TOOK THE BISCUIT.

. . . and then I defeated the terrifying monster using only a teaspoon and half a banana. It's TRUE!

Their TALL TALES were called MYTHS AND LEGENDS — stories that played a very important part in Greek life, religion and thought. The myths came from an age when there was NO writing and HARDLY ANY TELEVISIONS — and were passed down through storytelling in theatres and by word of mouth.

There were so many amazing adventures that we'd need several books to tell them all. But here are some of the best-known . . .

Let's begin with **THE MINOTAUR**.

According to the legend, an Athenian prince called **THESEUS** travelled to the island of Crete to kill a **MAN-EATING MONSTER** called the Minotaur. It was **HALF-MAN** and **HALF-BULL** and kept in a **SCARY MAZE** called the **LABYRINTH**.

MINOTAUR

THESEUS

So if you're ever in one of those mazes made of hedges and you hear something going 'MOOOO!' around the next corner — RUN! It might **JUST** be a cow on a day out, but **YOU NEVER KNOW** . . .

Other famous ancient Greek legends include the tale of the great hero Odysseus who took on Polyphemus, a one-eyed, MAN-EATING (and probably CHILD-EATING, if he fancied a snack) giant called a cyclops!

One day the beast trapped ODYSSEUS and his men inside his cave and began NIBBLING AWAY at them ONE BY ONE. Clever Odysseus brought the giant WINE to make him FALL ASLEEP. Then he drove A RED-HOT STAKE into his one eye. OOOOOOH! That's got to sting.

CYCLOPS

ODYSSEUS AND HIS MATES

Odysseus and his men then escaped by tying themselves beneath some sheep that Polyphemus kept in his cave overnight. As the sheep left the cave the blinded monster checked their backs, but not their bellies. IN YOUR FACE, POLYPHEMUS, (literally).

One of the greatest legends of all was that of **HERAKLES** — known to the Romans as **HERCULES**. He was one of the many children of the king of the gods, Zeus (no pressure), although his mum was a regular human.

IMPORTANT NOTE!
Please note that just because Herakles became a legend for swiping fruit doesn't mean you should. If you want a banana, buy one. Got it?

HERAKLES

Herakles started young. As a baby he **STRANGLED TWO SNAKES** with his **BARE HANDS**. But hey, who **HASN'T** strangled two snakes with their bare hands when they were a baby, right?

When he grew up he performed 12 tasks — also known as "labours" — for a king called Eurystheus, including slaying **A NINE-HEADED WATER SERPENT**, kidnapping a terrifying **THREE-HEADED DOG THING** that guarded the underworld, and stealing some **APPLES** (which was harder than it sounds).

Another well-known legend is the story of **ICARUS** who was given a pair of wax and feather wings by his father. But he flew **TOO CLOSE TO THE SUN** and when the wax holding the wings together melted he fell into the sea and **DROWNED**.

ICARUS

So please be careful if you're ever given a pair of waxy wings for your birthday. It's probably best going for a fly on cloudy days. Oh, and **STAY AWAY** from water.

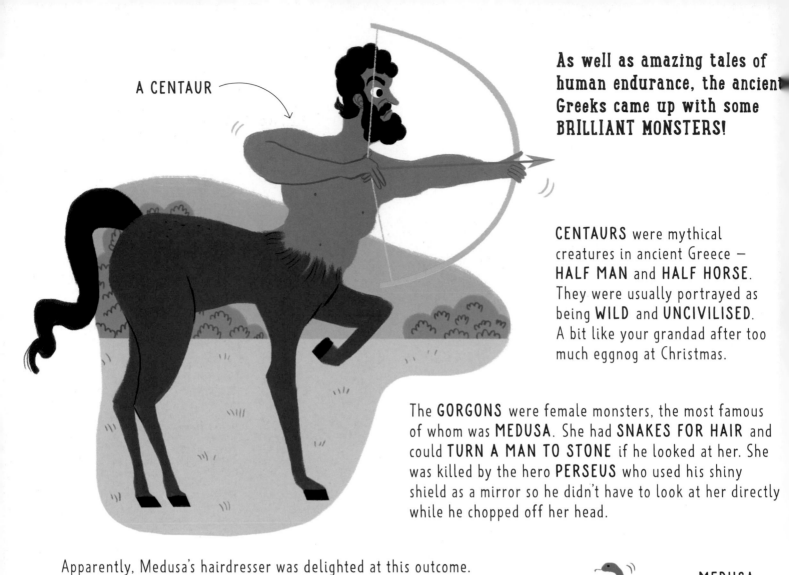

A CENTAUR

As well as amazing tales of human endurance, the ancient Greeks came up with some BRILLIANT MONSTERS!

CENTAURS were mythical creatures in ancient Greece — HALF MAN and HALF HORSE. They were usually portrayed as being WILD and UNCIVILISED. A bit like your grandad after too much eggnog at Christmas.

The GORGONS were female monsters, the most famous of whom was MEDUSA. She had SNAKES FOR HAIR and could TURN A MAN TO STONE if he looked at her. She was killed by the hero PERSEUS who used his shiny shield as a mirror so he didn't have to look at her directly while he chopped off her head.

Apparently, Medusa's hairdresser was delighted at this outcome. It was simply impossible to style those snakes into any kind of fashionable look, even with loads of hairspray.

MEDUSA
(Shield your eyes!)

FANCY THAT!

The ancient Greeks believed HARPIES were winged females who would fly down to steal children. To keep them away get a Harpy net, a tin of Harpy repellent and a rolled-up comic to swat them with.

HARPIES

Do you ever wish... you were magic?

Being able to disappear in a hurry could certainly come in handy — just after you've kicked a football through your gran's greenhouse, for example. But while the ancient Greeks might not have believed in the kind of magic that magicians in top hats and capes perform, they did set store in mysterious charms and curses ...

Curses that have been found inscribed on thin sheets of lead show that many people believed in magic and used it in everyday ancient Greek life.

Many of these curse tablets aren't very nice — they're based on jealousy or the hatred of someone for personal reasons. Several of them even call for revenge! Better not get on the wrong side of those grumpy ancient Greeks or you'll get a right good tableting!

"Magic" was also used to ward off evil, get rid of illness, attract good luck or make someone fall in love with you.

Ancient Greeks believed in witches, too. They had names like Circe and Medea, while the goddess of witches was called Hecate.

Hecate is often shown in images as three people standing back to back, as she is also the goddess of crossroads.

49

ANCIENT GREEK GODS

Sometimes it can be a real drag being told what to do all the time. Comb your hair! Tidy your room! Eat your greens!

Or even **WORSE**: Comb your room! Tidy your greens! Eat your hair!

There always seems to be someone above you, laying down the rules. Why can't they just **GET OFF YOUR CASE**, maaaaaan?

But if you think *YOU'VE* **GOT IT BAD**, at least your mum, dad or teachers don't throw **LIGHTNING BOLTS** around or have **LEGS LIKE A GOAT** — although Ms Krankhammer the head teacher **ALWAYS** wears trousers — so it's kind of hard to be sure . . .

The ancient Greeks had a whole load of gods keeping an eye on them — and they could be **DOWNRIGHT ODD** at times.

While the Greeks believed their gods had great powers, they also thought they had human qualities. Not only did they **FALL IN LOVE** and **GET MARRIED**, they also had children, sometimes with normal **MORTALS** (that's what you are, in case you were wondering). They also fell out with each other, **BIG STYLE**.

The highest mountain in Greece, **MOUNT OLYMPUS**, was believed to be the home of the gods.

Do you ever wish . . .
people gave you loads of presents?

If it's gifts you're after, you should probably consider becoming an ancient Greek god. They got LOADS of pressies! But maybe not the kind you'd want — unless a dead sheep is top of your birthday wish list?

Ancient Greek gods weren't all peaceful and chilled out. They could be angry, violent, jealous and turn super nasty if they got out of the wrong side if the bed in the morning.

To keep those grumpy old gods in a chirpy mood, the ancient Greeks would offer them prayers and, most importantly, sacrifices. The highest offering was a bull but they also offered other animals, such as goats and sheep, as well as other kinds of food and wine.

Sacrifices usually took place at an altar in front of a temple, with the people who were there eating the meat and inner bits and bobs of the animal after it was killed. Yummy — fresh entrails for lunch!

Liquid offerings, called "libations", were also commonly made, although it's unlikely these included lemonade, banana milkshakes or ice cream floats.

So, which ancient Greek god was the top dog, and who was lower down the pecking order?

ZEUS

HERA

ZEUS was the **KING OF THE GODS**, and is usually shown as a **STRONG MAN** with a **BIG BEARD**. He was the controller of **THUNDER** and **LIGHTNING**. He was married to his sister **HERA**, which is **PRETTY WEIRD**, so let's just park that there. Move along. Nothing to see here.

Things could get awfully odd when it came to old Zeus, it has to be said.

METIS

A painting on one vase shows the **STRANGE** birth of the goddess **ATHENA**, daughter of Zeus and his cousin, **METIS** (let's not go into that one, either).

Knowing that Metis might be carrying his child, Zeus **ATE HER**, because he was worried that any child born to Metis would be more powerful than he was.

Which seems **A BIT** of an **OVERREACTION**, if we're being honest. Hang on. It gets **BETTER**.

After that, Zeus ordered the god **HEPHAESTUS** to **CUT OPEN HIS HEAD** with a special axe he'd made, and out popped Athena, fully-grown and wearing armour!

Ta-dah!

ATHENA

MAGIC AXE

How's that for a magic trick? Sure beats pulling a **RABBIT OUT OF A HAT**.

As for the other gods, some could be **REAL MEANIES**.

ARTEMIS was the **GODDESS OF WILD ANIMALS** — probably more of the wolf and bear variety than bunnies and sparrows, judging by what she got up to. She was occasionally seen as a **VIOLENT GODDESS**, and caused the hunter **ACTAEON** to be torn apart by his own hounds because he had seen her **NAKED**!

ARTEMIS

I totally, 100 per cent did not see even a tiny bit of your bottom, Ms Goddess. And I don't have any dogs, just a gerbil and a couple of goldfish, so don't get any ideas.

ACTAEON
(who may have accidentally seen too much)

The ancient Greeks seemed to have a god for pretty much every occasion! After all, everyone needs a god of wine, a god of dreams and a god of fire, right?

EROS

EROS, the Greek GOD OF LOVE, is often depicted as a small child, sometimes with wings. He CARRIED A BOW and was thought to stir up feelings of love in humans by SHOOTING ARROWS at them.

A little kid? Shooting people with arrows? Errr, has anyone CALLED THE POLICE? That tiny dude needs to be LOCKED UP.

IMPORTANT NOTE!

Shooting someone you like with ANYTHING (especially sharp, pointy things) is just NOT ON! Try shooting them a smile instead.

One of the most unusual gods was PAN, the GOD OF FLOCKS and PROTECTOR OF SHEPHERDS. He had a human body but the LEGS, EARS AND HORNS OF A GOAT! That sounds like a BAAAA-D LOOK. He was believed to possess such a terrifying screech that it could paralyse animals with fear and topple city walls.

His name gives us the modern word "panic", but not the modern word "pants" – goats don't wear pants. We've checked.

PAN

HERMES

Do you ever wish... you had cool powers and super skills?

If the greatest powers you possess are the ability to be late for school every day and a talent for making chocolate biscuits disappear in the blink of an eye, you might fancy some of the skills the Greek gods had.

For instance, Zeus could toss out earth-shattering thunderbolts without even breaking sweat, and he could transform into other things, such as swans and bulls.

Poseidon, the god of the sea, had the ability to control water. So you'd never have to turn another tap on in your life — just click your fingers and the bath would be filled.

The god of war, Ares (who nobody liked) rode a chariot drawn by four fire-breathing stallions. Now that beats a new skateboard any day.

Hephaestus was the god of craftsmen and blacksmiths and created incredible robots such as three-legged tables that could move about and a giant bronze man called Talos. The school bully would think twice if you had a ginormous metal robot as a pal!

All these powers sound pretty awesome ... the only problem is that if you possessed them you'd probably have to become a god. And that sounds like a WHOLE lot of work and hassle, so maybe it's best just to stick to making choccie biccies mysteriously vanish?

FUN AND GAMES

Given everything you've read so far, it might sound as if ancient Greece was a terrible place, full of BLOOD SOUP, clothes coloured by SQUISHED-UP BABY BUGS and screeching gods with little HAIRY GOAT LEGS.

But it wasn't all DOOM AND GLOOM and CURDLED-MILK pancakes. There was plenty of fun to be had — if you had the time.

Although there isn't a huge amount of written information about ancient Greek childhood, clues can be found in objects discovered by archaeologists and in pictures painted on pottery that survives to this day.

For instance, one painting from a wine jug shows two young boys pulling their friend in what looks like a GO-KART!

FANCY THAT!

One popular game involved trying to hit a stone target by throwing things at it. If your throw landed the furthest away, you had to try to reach the target blindfolded while giving another player a piggyback. Give them a break — they didn't have *Minecraft* in those days.

Greek children often played with clay figurines, including a surviving one which shows a person RIDING A GOOSE. They were brightly painted and then placed in the graves of children to keep them company in the afterlife.

There were lots of other familiar games and toys that ancient Greek kids enjoyed. HOOPS, SPINNING TOPS, YO-YOS, ROCKING HORSES, SWINGS, SEE-SAWS, DOLLS and DOLLS' HOUSES were popular. PLAYSTATIONS, LAPTOPS and 3D MOVIES hadn't really caught on yet.

Many Greek girls enjoyed playing KNUCKLEBONES, which were very like modern jacks. They were made from the ankle joints of goats and the like. If you're ever passing a farm and see a goat giving you a worried look, perhaps he just thinks you're an ancient Greek after his knucklebones!

Watch your knuckles!

Children also played a MORE ENERGETIC version of "HEADS OR TAILS" – which actually sounds like a lot of fun. Kids would divide into two teams then toss up a piece of broken pottery called a "potsherd". Depending on which side up it landed, one team would chase the other and try to capture its members.

Why don't you give it a go? Just don't use your grandma's favourite china vase for the potsherd. Or if you do, don't tell anyone we gave you the idea . . .

If music is your thing, you're in luck — the ancient Greeks loved singing and played a wide variety of musical instruments, including the harp, lyre and the pan pipes.

Almost **NO WRITTEN MUSIC** has survived from the period, so no one knows what it sounded like. Maybe they were into **HIP HOP** and **HEAVY METAL?**

It seems women **ENJOYED A BOOGIE**, as there are many vase paintings showing women and girls dancing.

Men also enjoyed a turn on the dancefloor. Soldiers did something called **PHYRRHIC DANCE** dressed in **FULL ARMOUR**, and men also danced in theatre performances and at **MALE BEAUTY CONTENTS**. Just keep your fingers crossed **YOUR DAD** doesn't get any ideas!

Rich Greeks obviously had **MORE TIME AND MONEY** for fun — especially men. They held **DINNER PARTIES**, visited the **GYMNASIUM**, **WATCHED PLAYS** and enjoyed **GAMES**. But most women, poor Greeks, farmers and slaves had little time for leisure activities.

Although there **WEREN'T MANY CINEMAS** around, **THEATRES** were very popular. Ancient Greek theatres were amazing places, often carved out of hillsides, and could be **ENORMOUS**. The theatre at Epidauros could seat **14,000 PEOPLE!** All the actors were men who wore masks.

SOCRATES

As well as all that fun, ancient Greece had some of the **GREATEST THINKERS** the world has ever known — like **SOCRATES**, **PLATO** and **ARISTOTLE**.

So it seems life could be **JUST DANDY**, some of the time at least. Even if they **DID** very occasionally EAT PELICANS.

FANCY THAT!

Despite being one of the greatest thinkers of all time, the philosopher Socrates was accused of corrupting young people and sentenced to death by poison, all because some of the people in charge didn't like his ideas!

STILL THINK YOU'VE GOT IT BAD?

We hope you've had a blooming brilliant time on your tour of ancient Greece, and now you know all about what those cheeky Greeks got up to – do you *STILL* think YOU'VE GOT IT BAD?

YOU DO? *REALLY?*

OK, modern life can be tough at times. **ESPECIALLY** for kids.

Sometimes you have to put a cup in **THE DISHWASHER** and you don't **EVEN** get paid for doing it! Don't your parents realise you're not a **BUTLER?**

Or you're made to finish an **ENTIRE** plate of **SPAGHETTI BOLOGNAISE**, even though you specifically requested it without any bits in it **AT ALL**. What part of **"COMPLETELY SMOOTH SAUCE"** don't they understand?

But hey, at least you don't have to **EAT BLOOD SOUP**, live on **A MOUNTAIN** wearing **NOTHING** but a cloak, learn a poem that is **15,693 LINES LONG** or get married to someone you've never met when you're **JUST 13**.

Even without all that, some of the ancient Greek monsters alone are enough to give you **NIGHTMARES**. Unless you **REALLY** like snakes. The kind that grow out of people's heads. In which case, you're clearly a bit of a weirdo, so it doesn't count.

Next time you're tempted to have a little **WHINY-WHINE** about how **AAAAWFUL** life is in the 21st century, just take a moment to remember that even if you think you've got it bad . . . **you really don't!**

GLOSSARY

You may have noticed — if you've **REALLY** been paying attention — that not everything in this book is, strictly speaking, a fact. Actually, a few bits and bobs are plain made up just to make you chuckle. For example, there were **NO** televisions back then, Medusa **DIDN'T** have a hairdresser and there were definitely **NO** hot-water bottles or teddy bears in Sparta.

But aside from a few little giggle-bites like those, everything else is **100 PER CENT, SOLID-GOLD FACT!** Here are some more things to squeeze into your brainbox — if there's any room left . . .

ALEXANDER THE GREAT

Alexander was a king of the ancient Greek kingdom of Macedon. He spent most of his time in power leading his armies through Asia and northeast Africa to create one of the largest empires of the ancient world by the age of 30. Not to be confused with Alexander the OK-ish, who conquered an area the size of his back garden. In fact, it was his back garden.

ALTAR

Usually a platform or mound where people perform religious ceremonies or where sacrifices are offered to gods and ancestors. You could try popping a half-eaten doughnut on a chest of drawers as an offering to your great-great-great-great-great-great-grandad.

AMULET

Amulets were charms or pouches that were worn somewhere on the body — often round the neck. It was believed they had magical powers to protect the wearer from evil. You may wear a scarf around your neck, but that has no magical powers and will only protect you from a chilly breeze, not evil.

APOLLO

Apollo was a very important god. He was the son of Zeus and Leto, and had a twin sister called Artemis (the one who had the hunter chomped by his own dogs). He was a god of music, truth and prophecy, healing, the sun and light, plague, poetry, and more. What a busy god! When did he ever get time to watch his fave cartoons on TV?

ATHENA

Believed to have been born from the head of her father, Zeus (perfectly normal, nothing to see here, move along now). She was both the patron of craft and weaving *and* a warrior goddess believed to lead soldiers into battle. So, she could make you fight in a war, but she'd knit you a lovely helmet before you went.

BUCEPHALUS

Alexander the Great's horse was said to be a huge animal with an enormous head, a black coat and a large white star on his forehead. Alexander won Bucephalus in a wager — he bet a horse dealer he could tame the wild animal and surprised everyone by doing just that. Why not try winning a gerbil by betting a pet shop that you can tame the terrifying beast?

HOMER

He's that dim-witted yellow guy from *The Simpsons*. Hang on — we've already done that joke. Of course he isn't. The brainy Homer was the author of epic poems that told great stories. Or at least that's what some scholars say. Others think the poems were the work of several people, not one man. Check your shed for a time machine and you can go and see who's right.

LEECH

Leeches are a type of worm with two suckers, one at each end. Medicinal leeches, the kind that were used to suck blood by the Greeks, have three jaws that look like little saws with about 100 sharp teeth! Large adults can consume up to 10 times their body weight in blood in a single meal. Yikes! Just be thankful you don't get leeches the size of a cow.

LYRE

A musical instrument often made from a turtle shell, with two curved arms and strings stretched across its body. It was usually used to accompany someone singing a song. A lovely instrument adored by everyone except turtles. Unlikely to be used by many pop bands nowadays.

LABYRINTH

In Greek mythology, the labyrinth was a complicated maze built for King Minos of Crete at Knossos. It was created to hold the Minotaur, a beast with the body of a man and the head of a bull, which was eventually killed by the hero Theseus. If you're ever in one of those hedge mazes and you hear a grumpy "MOO", run.

LAURION SILVER MINES

Laurion was an area near the east coast of Greece. It was rich in silver, which the Athenians mined heavily, making their city very wealthy. The mines were active for thousands of years. There were about 350 mines worked by 10-20,000 slaves. The most you're likely to find digging in your back garden is a rusty toy car, lots of rocks and an old cat poo, so don't get your hopes up.

MYCENEANS

The Mycenaeans were the first advanced civilization in mainland Greece. They had grand palaces, organised societies, beautiful works of art and a system of writing. They introduced engineering innovations and traded over wide areas. Sounds like they were very clever — except their civilisation died out around 1100 BC, so, ummm . . .

PERSEUS

Perseus was a great Greek hero and slayer of monsters — ooooooooh, cool! He beheaded Medusa, which must have stung a bit, and saved Andromeda from the sea monster Cetus, which was awfully nice of him. He was the son of the powerful god Zeus, so he probably always tidied his room and ate his greens to keep on his dad's good side.

RIVER STYX

The Greeks believed that the Styx was a river which flowed seven times round the world of the dead. In ancient mythology it forms the boundary between Earth and the Underworld, which is often called *Hades*. To be honest, where water is concerned, you're probably best just sticking to your local swimming pool.

SANCTUARY

Sanctuaries were sacred places the ancient Greeks went to commune with their gods. It was separate from the outside, mortal world. Inside the sanctuary, sacrifices were performed and festivals were held. Everything inside belonged to the god. So if you ever go to one, don't take your favourite skateboard . . .

SOCRATES

One of the greatest thinkers ever, Socrates lived from about 470 to 399 BC. He was famous for asking lots of questions of his fellow Athenians. He was forced to drink poison because Athens' rulers at the time did not like his ideas. Bit extreme, guys — forcing him to drink a cup of fish guts or cow dribble would have been quite enough.

TRIREME

This was a fast, manoeuvrable warship powered by three levels of oarsmen — up to 170 in total. Many triremes had bronze-covered battering rams at the front, which made them fearsome weapons. Perfect for livening up a dull trip to the boating pond at your local park. Pedalo ahead — CHARGE!

INDEX